THE NIGHT BEFORE
CHRISTMAS

Clement C. Moore

THE NIGHT BEFORE CHRISTMAS

Illustrated by Robert Ingpen

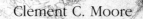

t
templar publishing

A TEMPLAR BOOK

Frist published in the UK in 2014 by Templar Publishing,
an imprint of Kings Road Publishing, part of the Bonnier Publishing Group,
The Plaza, 535 King's Road, London, SW10 0SZ
www.bonnierpublishing.com

Illustrations © 2010 Robert Ingpen
Design and layout © 2011 Palazzo Editions Ltd
Jacket cover design © 2014 by The Templar Company Limited

Art Director: Bernard Higton

3 5 7 9 10 8 6 4

ISBN: 978-1-78370-183-4

A CIP catalogue record for this book is available from the British Library.

Printed and bound in Singapore by Imago.

Originally created and produced by PALAZZO EDITIONS LTD,
15 Church Road, London, SW13 9HE
www.palazzoeditions.com

CLEMENT CLARKE MOORE
(1779–1863)

DR. Clement C. Moore was born in New York City in 1779, and lived his whole life in the same large house in Manhattan, Chelsea House (the area that surrounded it is now known as the Chelsea District, after the Moore home.) He was one of New York's wealthiest and most educated men, and had a deep love of language. He was best known in his day as a professor of Greek and Oriental literature at Columbia College, and his greatest scholarly achievement was writing a Hebrew dictionary, the first of its kind to appear in America. But he also loved to write stories and poems for his nine children.

On Christmas Eve in 1822, when the Moore children had hung up their stockings ready for Santa Claus, their father entertained them with the poem he had penned for them as a Christmas present. The story, which began with the immortal words, "Twas the night before Christmas…" was later written down for the children, who memorized and recited it for friends and family. A family friend who heard it sent a copy to the editor of a New York newspaper, the *Troy Sentinel*, where it was printed anonymously the following Christmas with the title, *A Visit From St. Nicholas*. It then appeared in a magazine, and was soon being translated into numerous languages and even into Braille.

Clement C. Moore's timeless poem, which perfectly captures the magic and anticipation of Christmas Eve, is now irrevocably an essential part of the build-up to Christmas for countless families. It is a delight to read aloud, and is recited to excited children all over the world every Christmas Eve, a fact that would probably amuse its serious, respected academic author!

'Twas the night before Christmas,
when all through the house
Not a creature was stirring,
not even a mouse.

The stockings were hung
    by the chimney with care,
In hopes that St. Nicholas
    soon would be there.

The children were nestled
all snug in their beds,
While visions of sugarplums
danced in their heads.

And Mama in her 'kerchief,
and I in my cap,
Had just settled down
for a long winter's nap.

When out on the lawn
　　there arose such a clatter,
I sprang from the bed
　　to see what was the matter.

Away to the window
I flew like a flash,
Tore open the shutters
and threw up the sash.

The moon on the breast
of the new-fallen snow
Gave the luster of midday
to objects below,

When, what to my wondering eyes
    should appear,
But a miniature sleigh,
    and eight tiny reindeer,

With a little old driver,
so lively and quick,
I knew in a moment
it must be St. Nick.

More rapid than eagles
his coursers they came,
And he whistled, and shouted,
and called them by name:

"Now, Dasher! Now, Dancer!
Now, Prancer and Vixen!
On, Comet! On, Cupid!
On, Donder and Blitzen!"

"To the top of the porch!
To the top of the wall!
Now, dash away! Dash away!
Dash away all!"

As dry leaves that before
the wild hurricane fly,
When they meet with an obstacle,
mount to the sky.

So up to the house-top
   the coursers they flew,
With the sleigh full of toys—
   and St. Nicholas too.

And then, in a twinkling,
I heard on the roof
The prancing and pawing
of each little hoof.

As I drew in my head,
and was turning around,
Down the chimney St. Nicholas
came with a bound.

He was dressed all in fur,
from his head to his foot,
And his clothes were all tarnished
with ashes and soot.

A bundle of toys
he had flung on his back,
And he looked like a peddler
just opening his pack.

His eyes—how they twinkled!
His dimples how merry!
His cheeks were like roses,
his nose like a cherry!

His droll little mouth
was drawn up like a bow.
And the beard on his chin
was as white as the snow!

The stump of a pipe
he held tight in his teeth.
And the smoke it encircled
his head like a wreath.

He had a broad face
and a little round belly,
That shook when he laughed,
like a bowlful of jelly.

He was chubby and plump,
   a right jolly old elf,
And I laughed when I saw him,
   in spite of myself.

A wink of his eye
and a twist of his head,
Soon gave me to know
I had nothing to dread.

He spoke not a word,
   but went straight to his work,
And filled all the stockings,
   then turned with a jerk.

And laying his finger
aside of his nose,
And giving a nod,
up the chimney he rose.

He sprang to his sleigh,
   to his team gave a whistle,
And away they all flew
   like the down of a thistle.

But I heard him exclaim
   as he drove out of sight,
"Merry Christmas to all,
   and to all a good night!"